I0158132

How To
Improve Your Characters
To Improve Your
Sci-Fi Story.

Don Foxe
donfoxe.com

CABALLUS
PRESS™

Copyright © 2018 don foxe

Printed in the United States of America

ISBN: 9781732103641

Written by Don Foxe. donfoxe.com

Produced by Caballus Press, USA Division
www.caballuspress.com

Stock images are used for illustrative purposes only.
Some stock imagery from Pixabay.com, Unsplach.com, and Stock-Adobe.com
Model image on cover used with permission.

Acknowledgements:

bfi.org.uk for sci-fi films information
editing-writing.com - articles on writing fiction
io9.gizmodo.com - articles on Sci-Fi Characters
thecreativepenn.com - articles on writing
writerswrite.com - character profile forms

INTRODUCTION

Having a good story to tell is key to success. Having characters to tell the story are the keys to the kingdom. Characters readers (watchers & listeners) believe, become attached to, and care about unlock the imagination.

As a writer, I start with a story. I insert a main character whose job is to follow the trail of action, intrigue, romance, and adventure considered a plot. Along the way this main character must interact with others. Some assist the protagonist, some attempt to prevent their continued forward motion, and some are simply scene setters. Eventually the main character reaches the end of the story -- the climax.

I have given my lead character the qualities necessary for him or her to succeed. I have, hopefully, also provided the characteristics to make them interesting. I do not care if my reader relates to the character. They do not have to like him or her or it. But they must be engaged.

Like most writers, I began as a reader. Living in these times also means experiencing sci-fi through television, movies, comic books, and games. All of these experiences work together to lead me to a style of science fiction writing I am most comfortable producing. The Space Opera and Military Science Fiction formats fit my needs. These are subcategories filled with authors, great, good, and bad. My love for world building, the pursuit of research to support my theories, and the amount of history, especially military-conflict history keep me entertained.

Developing characters requires work.

For fun, I made a list of my favorite characters from television and movies. No particular order, just the first ten that came to mind:

The Doctor, Doctor Who
Ellen Ripley, Alien
Darth Vader, Star Wars
Captain Malcolm Reynolds, Firefly / Serenity
HAL-9000, 2001: A Space Odyssey
Rick Deckard, Blade Runner
Han Solo, Star Wars
Spock, Star Trek
Buck Rogers
Terminator

With the Doctor, my enjoyment waxes and wanes with the different actors. My love of the series is based on the relentless fight to save humanity against outside forces, even if saving humanity is a questionable pursuit.

That Ripley is the only female that immediately came to mind bothers me. There are several female characters I consider important, usually vital to the outcome, in my own books.

Two machines. Hal and the Terminator. Single-minded and driven, regardless of obstacles. Devoid of mercy. Intelligent without emotional complications. How often have I wished I could conduct some interpersonal or business decision without the entanglements of humanity?
Two bad guys: Vader and Terminator.

One straight-up hero: Buck Rogers.

Three reluctant heroes with issues: Reynolds, Deckard, and Solo.

One side-kick: Spock.

All fighters. All flawed. All struggling with inner-demons. All hiding those demons from others.

Wondering if my fascination with reluctant heroes and superior villains, I jotted down sci-fi books with characters I wish I knew more about. Books I re-read in hopes of discovering more about the people, not the plot.

Paul Atreides: **DUNE** by Frank Herbert
Severian: **The Book of the New Sun** by Gene Wolfe
Mannie: **The Moon is a Harsh Mistress** by Robert Heinlein
Raul Endymion: **Endymion** and **The Rise of Endymion**
Case and Molly: **Neuromancer** by William Gibson

My first piece of advice to you, sci-fi writer or wannabe, is consider what characters move you as a reader, watcher, or listener. Does not have to be in sci-fi related works. Do not do this so you reinvent a character already made famous. Try to understand your own fascination with characters. If the characters in your writing interest you, your writing will become more interesting.

The first character that comes to mind is

What about this person intrigues you?

SECTION ONE: CHARACTERS ESTABLISH THE ATTITUDES YOUR READERS MUST EMBRACE.

By default your vision of the world your story is set within will be different from the world of your readers. Whether it is a different version of Earth, or another world altogether, for your tale to survive the first few chapters without the reader tossing it aside, they must be convinced your concept it possible; perhaps probable.

You could spend pages and pages describing your world, or worse, how your world came to be. This exposition will be covered later, but for now I simply suggest DON'T. You may be fascinated with the universe you built within your head. I assure you attempting to explain the details will bore others to tears.

If you want to show the reader this world is possible, do so by your characters' attitudes toward their reality. To the reader, everything will be unfamiliar. Some things will be strange. Most things will be new. Everything needs to be exciting. To your characters, this world is ho-hum. A ship is under construction on an orbital platform in space. The platform is home to thousands of people. These characters live, work, and play here every day, and have for some time. Perhaps they are third or fourth generation. Their attitudes toward your introduction to this new vision of life is your way to describe what is considered normal, and what may be new and different.

You have an entire novel, perhaps, as I prefer, an entire space opera to bring out the details of your mythology. Do not shove it in the reader's mind's eye.

Writer Tip:

With science-fiction especially, you need to stand out quickly if you expect someone to buy your book. This means your introduction must be exciting, gripping, and filled with suspense. Because most people today sample before they buy, and samples are the first couple of chapters, at most, you need to be prepared for that reality.

When I tell you to introduce your world as believable through the conversations and actions of the characters living within that world, that begins AFTER you hook the imagination.

Creating Characters and Assigning Attitudes

You know the story you want told. You know how you want to relate some truth; some final outcome. You have a vision of the future (usually), and you really want to share that vision. To accomplish your goal readers need to become engaged. We do not become empathetic to scenery, no matter how wondrous. We do not relate to technology, regardless of its potential to change our life. In spite of all the experts telling us how social media is destroying human interaction, humans crave communication. We need interaction. We need characters in our lives.

Take your time to craft all of your characters. You must invest yourself in creating truly engaging, amazing, believable, and sustainable characters. When you decide to tell a story set in a world alien to your readers, it is essential for them to relate with your characters. Yes, even the alien and altered.

I did not write fiction for thirty-years because I spent too much time reading how to write fiction by experts. When I simply sat down and wrote my story, it flowed out of my head and into my document saver. I am a stream-of-conscious writer. I know others, really fantastic authors, who must storyboard, outline, and predetermine their plots. I cannot do that. They cannot write without a guide. I cannot color inside the lines. You must find your own path.

What I did learn is my story, regardless of how entertaining, needed a lot of rewriting to become worthy of publication. Unfortunately, with digital publishing and self-publishing, a lot of books reach the markets. Some are fantastic. Most are horrid. Horrid because the writer published what I would consider a rough draft. You decide what your name goes on. In my case, I rewrite to improve my characters. I rewrite to work my research into technology and possible future technologies into my stories. I rewrite after I have others I trust read my rough story and tell me their concerns. I even rewrite after my editor corrects spelling and grammar.

Mostly I rewrite to make damn sure my characters remain true.

Just as in how you write, there is no right method to create characters. For your characters to be empathetic, believable, or horrifying they require layers. It is easy to rely on stereotypes when creating characters. It is simple to describe them physically, give them the traits you need them to have for your plot-line, and leave the rest to imagination. Simple and lazy.

I told you I write stream-of-thought. I also am extremely organized. I have notebooks on the technology I present in Space Fleet Sagas. I also have complete, detailed volumes on characters; major, minor, and potential. Volumes which do not remain static. As characters interact with new situations, with new characters, they evolve. I note these changes.

I have back-stories on every character. Some detailed, and some basic outlines. Some of this information works its way into my books. Most is used to keep me connected to my characters so the reader gets to know them by their actions, not because I detail their life story. Actions taken because of who they are and how they would act in any given situation based on their history.

Do you need to be this detailed? Perhaps not. But you need to consider being more engaged with your own creations if you expect others to do the same.

When I write, and especially when I rewrite, I keep an index card with the character's name and two columns on a board near my computer. This allows me to check myself to see if I remain true to my character within the story. The index cards are specific to each new book.

The information is in Don short-hand as reminders. If I need to check something more deeply, I go to a character's pages in one of my journals.

The right-side column has:

Goal: (What this character's goal is to accomplish by the end of the story.)
Wants and needs: (What they want to happen; what they need to get it.)
Likes and dislikes: (Basics regarding dealing with others.)

These represent the most basic layers of their character.

The left-side column gets more involved:

Worst fear: What really drives this person to succeed.

Desires: What they really want, not what they pretend to want.

Beliefs: Moral Compass - what are they willing to do to win.

Situations in your story should be designed to expose your characters. How they deal with these situation will reveal their natures. Make sure they deal with things according to the traits you have assigned them. There is always room for ambiguity. There is always an opportunity to make a decision that goes against character. But these must be the exception, otherwise they lose importance. Major characters dealing with contradictions help make a story feel real. This is something everyone experiences. We all face times when we decide to do something that is uncomfortable. Sometimes regrettable. When we are lucky, by acting against our better judgment, we actually create a better outcome.

These situations place the needs and desires of a character into the forefront. The protagonist will always accept what they want over what they secretly need. At some point, the protagonist must become aware of his or her needs. They must decide to either change in order to fulfill those needs, or turn their back on personal desire for the larger goal. That action, and those changes lead to the protagonist's character arc.

Character Arcs

If a character changed during the story, the character experienced a character arc. The protagonist, the main character driving the story, should be your most layered character. As the plot continues, the protagonist's character arc occurs gradually. By the end, the protagonist is a different person, transformed by the events in the novel. Are they a better person? Not always. Are they changed forever? In some ways, but they have the ability to regain themselves, or relapse to a worse version in later stories.

Major characters should go through a character arc. How great of an arc is up to you. There are many different types of character arcs.

Examples from my own books would include Daniel Cooper recognizing his need to act alone, without the restraints of authority or the responsibilities of a crew. Another example is the redemption of an anti-hero. Captain Amanda Black is introduced as a character who embodies greed, lust for power, and the inability to handle command. In later books we find out she was out of her element. A secret agent for the good guys caught up in the moment. She goes from incompetent villain in Book One to hero in Book Five.

Readers love bad guys. A villain, who does not have to be the antagonist to your protagonist, requires as many layers as the protagonist. A villain who does bad deeds without an objective or a plan, is single-dimensional. Remember, evil people NEVER perceive themselves as evil. This quirk alone provides a writer with limitless ideas as to what really motivates evil acts.

Science fiction as a genre often deals with grand ideas, where the opposite force might be a government, a corporation, a council, an opposing alien race, and so on. Because of that reason, you need to find the characters within the opposing forces who can be the face of the enemy – or the villain. And even in that case, the villain character needs a specific reason as to why he or she become the enemy in the story.

Character Relationships

The relationships between characters is vital in a science fiction story. Every situation can raise the danger levels for each character. You can also raise the potential for losses and gains in relationships between the characters. I once read a suggestion that every chapter, every paragraph should contain the threat of imminent death. Writing as if everything and anyone could be destroyed at any moment added a thrill for the reader.

If every character gets along, or simply stay in their stereotypical lanes, you have no drama. Any dramatic plot depends heavily on imperfect relationships between the characters. This conflicts created the original Greek dramas. As the characters in your tale go through their character arcs, there should be a similar change in their personal relationships.

Every reader has experienced these changes. When we go from child to adult, not only do how we think and act evolve, so do the relationships between us and our parents, siblings, and friends.

Breaking up with a girlfriend or boyfriend is life-changing . . . at the time. Characters should feel dramatic changes deeply, even if we all know things will even out with time.

Introducing imperfect character relationships adds drama. Dealing with diverse personalities adds obstacles for the protagonist to overcome. But do not go overboard! The protagonist's first goal is to reach the climax and experience personal changes that come with attaining his or her goal. The relationships with other major and minor characters should be treated as side plots. These are plot threads which could lead somewhere, but in the immediacy of the story, they add to the protagonist's view of him-herself, and almost always a change in their nature.

Character Tropes and Stereotypes

A trope is a recurrent theme. Unassuming and unknown person rises to defeat the all powerful enemy and save the day. A stereotype is oversimplifying a person by placing them within an image generally regarded as fact. The Asian who is bright, but awkward in social situations.

It is important to note one thing: when you create a character, it is not wrong to rely on a trope for the first layer of the character. Failing to add depth to the character as the story progresses is where writers often goes astray. For example, it is okay for a female love interest to be Mary Ann or Ginger at the beginning – however, that character remaining a stereotype will cause the reader to lose interest. You must add depth. Why are they the way they are? Are they what they appear? What will make them change?

The same thing applies to all major characters in your novel.

Some types of characters have become common in science fiction:

– The cannon fodder characters: characters who appear (some are even named) before a major event where people die – including the newly met characters. The poor Red-shirt uniform Star Trek crew members on their first Away Mission.

– The writer's voice character: This poor soul acts as the author's mouthpiece. The easiest way for a writer to educate the reader is via this character. Someone who delivers world building information to the readers. They often talk about the science and technology of the era and its creation. The geek-quotient is often high and the character usually presented as socially awkward.

– The chosen one – the hero who will save the day. My personal favorite.

– The double-agent: the traitor. The surprise bad guy.

– The fake double-agent: the character who outwardly appears as a double agent, but is in fact far from it. The surprise good guy.

– The female love interest without any tangible connection with the protagonist but is often presented as the prize at the end of the novel.

There are many other character stereotypes in science fiction. Guess what? Every genre has its own long list of stereotypical characters. The goal of a good writer is to begin with the clay, but then sculpt layered characters. Subvert the stereotypes. Turn them around to the joy of your reader. A love interest should still come with a personality. Supply opinions, and introduce conflict with the protagonist. Anyone married for any length of time will relate.

All of these character traits, relationships, arcs, and changes must happen within the events of the dramatic plot. For me, these things become hashed out in the rewrites. In my first draft, characters are often simple stereotypes. My second draft is normally many thousands-of-words longer than my original. My next draft is when I cut out extraneous crap and pare characters down to the essentials necessary to the story.

SECTION TWO: DRAMA DEFINED THROUGH CHARACTERS

The Dramatic Plot in Science Fiction

The dramatic plot refers to plots and side plots related to the characters themselves, not just to the science or psychology you want to expound upon.

For readers to read your story and remain engaged so they eventually discover your hidden gems of wisdom, you need to make sure it is dramatic enough to catch and then hold their attention. You need conflict: between two people, two planets, two species, two galaxies -- you get the concept.

How do you put two things into conflict?

You choose your two characters, one from each side. Then you bring them together. Sounds incredibly simple. Conflict is always simple. Easiest thing that exists between two of anything. It is resolving conflict that takes effort.

If your characters are not black and white, but come with many layers, bringing them together will give you an even greater dramatic conflict. Even if that conflict is indirectly related to your main plot. Sometimes, the dramatic plot, the goal is related only to the protagonist. He or she may need to deal with old demons before being able to cope with new issues. They may be affected by the events of the main plot, but their personal internal struggles are one underlying theme of your story.

Introducing conflict is crucial to the progress of the story. The type of conflict tells the reader what you consider the important message of your novel. You may be

15

interested in only creating action and adventure, leaving social commentary to others. You may wish to provide both. Science fiction is one genre that fully allows such breadth of theme.

Do not confuse action with drama. The action within your story can create tension, apprehension, fear, and hope. Drama develops the backdrop. Drama increases all the emotions you want the reader to experience when action occurs.

Drama develops from dynamics within family interactions, romantic involvements, and friendships. Workplace drama? Who has not dealt with that?

Characters in science fiction can be and often are aliens. Usually portrayed as human-like. Human characteristics relative to their psychology, even if their physical appearance is not humanoid. Some Sci-Fi writers enjoy android-robotic-artificial intelligence characters. These also display human traits. Always remember humans are inherently flawed. The fatal flaw, the one trait one overlooks when self-analyzing, is the basis of tragedy. Overcoming that flaw leads to triumph.

Every major decision made by your protagonist should result from struggle. An inner conflict where there are no good choices. One side wins and the other loses. To remain loyal to a cause, the betrayal of friends or family may be required. To save a friend, a sacred oath must be shattered. Which way will your hero select? Will they remain true to their nature, or go against the grain? These internal conflicts apply to most major characters in your novel. Their decisions change their character and move the plot forward.

Your characters are human, even the non-humans. They had an existence, a life before your story begins.

They do not begin with a name written on a whiteboard in your office. They had friends, families, love interests, and dreams. This baggage should be brought along, introduced at the proper time within your story to add depth, and provide the drama necessary to make your character believable.

You should know their backstories. You do not need to share them. Just knowing what motivates a character can come through when you describe how they act when placed in conflict.

SECTION THREE: TAKE A BREAK!

Sub-genres.

Take a moment and walk away from character development. Instead, consider the multitude of Sci-Fi Sub-Genres. No one craves being locked into a corner, but you should decide if a specific subject mater within the literary universe of science fiction best describes your point of view. Your comfort zone.

From the literary aspect, science fiction is epic. The genre can be divided into dozens of sub-genres. Every smaller category comes with its own unique themes, while every one offers you the ability to cross imaginary lines. Like the wormholes in my own Space Fleet Sagas universe, many are known and used, and many remain uncharted. Finding a niche can help you better form your characters. It does not define you or them. Like any stereotype or trope, it provides a starting point.

HARD SCIENCE FICTION

Science and technology are the stars. Scientific concepts are explained in detail. Hard Sci-Fi is concept heavy, and attempts to provide scientific realism. Plot development is too often driven at the expense of character development.

SOFT SCIENCE FICTION

Now science and technology take a back-seat to character-driven plots. How things operate are less important than why they exist and how they impact life.

Hereafter, the categories are presented in alphabetical order. There is no better or best sub-genre. There is no good or bad choices for a writer in selecting a preference.

ALIEN CONSPIRACY

Fiction in which the existence of aliens has been hidden from the public by government officials.

ALIEN INVASION

Aliens attempt to invade the Earth. They come through military conquest, political subversion, or extraterrestrial-induced plague. The invasion can be to enslave or designed for mass extermination.

An interesting subversion is humans invading an alien world.

ALTERNATE HISTORY

Alternate history stories are placed in a world in which history has taken a different course. The time-line change is often the result of a single event, an *identifier,* that causes this change; the assassination of Hitler; Rome does not fall. When science or aliens intervene, the stories are sub-genre to Sci-Fi, otherwise, they may be better considered as speculative fiction works.

APOCALYPTIC SCIENCE FICTION

Fiction concerning a cataclysmic event. The decline of the human race, human extinction, societal upheaval, or the total destruction of the Earth.

BIOPUNK

Biopunk is similar to cyberpunk, except the main theme is the use of bio-technology and genetic engineering rather than computer technology. Genetic manipulation, body modification, and eugenics are common themes. Social decline and political repression are often the driving forces behind story lines.

CYBERPUNK

Fiction relating to the science of cybernetics. Nature is seen as a series of interconnecting mechanical systems. Specifically, cyberpunk deals with the links between biology and computer technology. The story explores humanity's changing relationship with computer systems. Virtual reality, prosthetics, cyborgs, and current social themes connected to the internet are all part of the cyberpunk niche - and social decline.

DYSTOPIAN FICTION

Dystopian fiction deals with political repression by police states. A dystopian society is one in which freedoms are limited and conventional morality has been perverted. This is the opposite of a utopian society. George Orwell's **1984** is the birth of dystopian fiction

EROTIC SCIENCE FICTION

Sexually explicit science fiction. With aliens, with other humans in space, with holograms, with robots, with . . . you get the idea.

FIRST CONTACT

Explores the results of humans meeting extra-terrestrials for the first time. The first contact could be friendly, harsh, or accidental.

GOTHIC SCIENCE FICTION

Gothic science fiction explores traditional gothic concepts (magic, monsters, etc.) and provides a scientific explanation. A good example of this would be vampirism explained as a rare blood disease. The abilities of ancient gods the work of advanced alien technology.

LOST WORLDS

Discovery of forgotten lands (islands, lost continents, isolated jungles, etc.). The subsequent discovery of scientific wonders (living dinosaurs, ancient technology, Shambala), and the dangers they present to the characters.

MILITARY SCIENCE FICTION

Characters are usually members of a military organization. The story will generally revolve around a war and/or military conflict. Duty, honor, heroism and other military themes are presented and explored. Research in military planning and strategy are as important for realism as research into the advanced technology displayed.

MUNDANE SCIENCE FICTION

Science fiction using only currently available or theoretical, but accepted, probable future technology. This usually discounts faster-than-light travel or anything outside the laws of physics. The aim is to create realism and explore science fiction ideas closer to home. Stories of exploration and colonization within in our own solar system are examples.

Mundane science fiction strives to promote a more realistic view of our universe so as to avoid future disillusionment associated with science fiction. It is hoped this will lead to an appreciation of the natural wonders and resources found on Earth, the moon, and those planets nearby.

NANOPUNK

Nanopunk is closely related to cyberpunk and biopunk. The three sub-genres sometimes combined. Nanopunk's focus is on the use of microscopic machinery (or nanotechnology).

PARALLEL WORLDS

Fiction concerning travel to parallel universes, in which the new world can be slightly to completely different from our own. The theory of parallel universes states that there are an infinite number of these alternate worlds, and an infinite number of potential stories. The traditional way to visit them is via a wormhole (or Einstein-Rosen bridge). In my urban fantasy serial, *Dúnmharú*, I employ plane-traveling through (so-far) unexplained gates that connect planets and dimensions.

POST-APOCALYPTIC FICTION

Fiction set in the aftermath of a cataclysmic event. The world and human civilization has been radically changed. Post-apocalyptic landscapes are usually depicted as grim, with survivors facing a multitude of dangers. Stories are filled with violence, starvation, radiation effects, extreme weather, and the often-required mutants.

RECURSIVE SCIENCE FICTION

Author Mike Resnick dubbed this as "science fiction about science fiction". More precisely, it is science fiction with multiple references to other Sci-Fi works. The writer, and the characters attempt to examine, parody, or pay homage to existing science fiction works. The television show **Orwell** could be considered a Recursive view of Star Trek.

RETRO FUTURISM

Retro futurism is the post-Art Deco 1950s American fascination with science fiction. Steampunk revitalized the works of Verne and Wells. Retro Futurism recaptures the spirit (or satirizes the campy nature) of the golden age of science fiction and stories such as **Forbidden Planet**.

ROBOT FICTION

Fiction with the science of robotics a central theme. Often relative issues to Isaac Asimov and the conflicts possible when advanced robotics and humans collide. The unintended consequences plot-line.

SCIENTIFIC ROMANCE

This term was used before someone came up with science fiction. It generally refers to the works of early British Sci-Fi writers like H.G Wells. It indicates a story of intrigue, exploration, discovery with a romanticized main character achieving scientific glory against all odds.

SCIFI/COMEDY

Science fiction that is humorous. Often satirical. SpaceBalls.

SCIFI/FANTASY

Sometimes called Science Fantasy, these stories include elements of both the science fiction and fantasy genres. Concepts traditionally belonging to science fiction (space travel, robots) appear alongside those associated with fantasy (magic, mythology). SteamPunk without the steam.

SCIFI/HORROR

Bridge the narrow divide between science fiction and horror genres. Basically, a good tale of horror set in a science fiction world. Often an unintended killer created or released by science.

SLIPSTREAM

I almost did not include Slipstream as a sub-genre because it is either a sub-genre of all types of fiction or a stand alone style. Slipstream's tendency toward the absurd is sometimes at odds with mainstream science fiction. The point of slipstream is to create a feeling of disillusionment. It questions your view of reality.

SOCIAL SCIENCE FICTION

Future or alien societies are extrapolated, explained, and placed under critical observation by the author. Writers with a purpose of social satire or a warning enjoy this sub-genre. Science and technology will play a major role in the structure of the extrapolated society, but how the society deals with advances is the main theme.

Speculative fiction, is the non-science fiction relative when science and technology are not central to the plot, or if the writer does not wish to be lumped in with science fiction authors.

SPACE OPERA

Space Opera is my personal domain, but I have never embraced the term. It is a confusing category in that it is too broad. It typically refers to long-running science fiction series with continuing story arcs. These are usually set in space, or involve travel between two or more planets. Space Operas present a large number of recurring characters and focus on large-scale fictional events, such as galactic conflicts between species.

Recurring themes in space opera include politics, imperialism, colonialism, war, space exploration, heroism, rebellion, or, if you prefer the short explanation -- everything within every other sub-genre in one location.

SPACE WESTERN

Science fiction in which a future space-flight-capable society is portrayed as being like that of the American West. The comparison may be literal, with western clothing and revolvers in stead of laser pistols. It may be figurative, depicting a lawless society of space pioneers. *Firefly*.

STEAMPUNK

Steampunk merges the science fiction with alternate history concepts. The design aesthetic of the 19th and early 20th Centuries provide the backdrop. It is a literary fiction, history, cultural style, and an artistic movement in a one-stop shop.

Steampunk (over-simplified) is the introduction of modern, or futuristic, concepts and technologies into an earlier setting. Or reverse gears and place an older culture, complete with dress and morays, into a technologically advanced world. It focuses largely on 'the age of steam' and the perceived inventiveness of industrial engineers. In a steampunk timeline advanced tech may have been created alongside early industrial-age inventions, or even powered by steam engines. Some Steam Punk writers even mix magic into the gumbo.

Since the 1980's steampunk has grown from a literary genre and into a large-scale artistic and cultural movement. Central to this movement is the belief that 19th Century literature (the works of Jules Verne and H.G Wells in particular), innovations, and fashion were more aesthetically appealing, and more durable than those produced by today's 'throw-away' culture.

It also provides awesome examples for Cosplay roles.

SUPERHERO FICTION

Is it a science fiction sub-genre? Is it fantasy? Is it a stand-alone literary device? Every person can make their own decision, and each is correct. The level of scientific realism displayed by the themes of your story (your super hero) affect the degree to which it is acceptable as science fiction.

TIME TRAVEL

Science fiction in which the character/characters travel into the past or future. These adventures often include themes from alternate history and parallel worlds sub-genres.

VOYAGES EXTRORDINAIRES

Before the term *science fiction* originated, Jules Verne used this term to categorize his works. *Extraordinary voyages* describes the exploratory format of his stories as well as the fantastical ideas they contain. Today, the term is assigned to works directly inspired by Verne, or which follow the same format and the same spirit of adventure.

ZOMBIE FICTION

Zombie fiction is also claimed by the horror and fantasy genres but it is considered science fiction at it core. A zombie-inspired story may fall into any one or more of these categories, depending on its content and theme. However, most zombie fiction occurs post-apocalyptic, set during or following a *zombie apocalypse*, and can be categorized under Sci-Fi or Sci-Fi-Horror.

Embrace your sub-genre. There is no shame in sharing an affection for a particular theme. You can always write multiple books and explore different themes.

One thing for a writer to consider is readers. Readers do tend to repeat read. If you have a strong grasp on the style of your story, it will help you when it comes time to market the published end result.

SECTION FOUR: EXPOSITION VIA CHARACTERS

My best beta-reader is my wife, Sarah. Sarah does not like science fiction. She has no need to watch a new Star Wars movie before it is available for television at home. She finds the genre tedious, so imagine how she feels about all those long-winded details regarding technology? That I feel required to provide substance to my futuristic advances, human or alien, does not change the fact that exposition, detailed descriptions, and explanations are BORING!

Not just science-based principles, but historical background, political organizations, geographical or spatial features. The wonders of spaceships can become tedious diatribes that may impress the sci-fi geek, but dissuade the average reader from plowing through until the next exciting part.

I spend hours on hours researching political and trade organizations, military aspects of strategy and planning, the aeronautics of in-atmosphere and space flight, and new discovers in physics. I cannot waste this research by not using it to validate my social constructs, conflicts, and futuristic capabilities for fight, flight, and life -- alien and otherwise. I also cannot upset my wife.

Using Sarah (thank God for her patience), I have rewritten and recreated scenes with over-powering expositions until they are short enough, or entertaining enough for her, and still fill my need for validation. The process required, and still requires, a lot of time. The effort has made me a much better writer.

It has also made me appreciate the need for layered characters, and to introduce characters capable of presenting details in more entertaining methods than *here they are.*

My first draft, as already said, is stream of thought. Because of this there will be sections where I either go into long detailed explanations of what something is, how it works, or why it exists as I perceive it. Sometimes I simply place a (PUT DETAILS HERE) note and move on with the story.

Either way, on rewrite, when I bump into these potential reader-killers, my first action is to decide if I have a character or characters who can present the details in a more conversational means.

ONE

Details can slow a story's pace, but those same details viewed through the characters can add interest. The opportunity exists to create a believable piece of futuristic innovation add realism to my mythological world because the character considers it normal (See Attitudes in Section One). I also get a chance to layer the character's personality. How they talk about the *thing,* and their opinions tell you more about their beliefs.

Two personal examples from my first Space Fleet Sagas book, **Contact and Conflict,** are the best way for me to example this.

After the exciting prelim, in the first chapter Captain Daniel Cooper is watching his new space ship, the PT-109, John F. Kennedy, prepared for its final breakdown voyage. My first time through I simply wrote all of the details about the ship: size, power plants, weapons, unique capabilities. In rewrite, as he stands there a young woman next to him begins to list the details like a gallery guide would run off aspects of a piece of art. Factual, but kind of cold. He does not know this young woman. Does not know how she knows so much about his ship. Distracted, when he looks back, she is gone. Foreshadowing and character building completed.

When readying his fighter to face an alien enemy, like any good pilot he performs a checklist with his alien-ally co-pilot. Details are still pretty dry, but the weapons and capabilities of the ship are detailed in an entertaining, believable way. The alien co-pilot gets to ask questions because many of these systems are, well, alien to her.

Two

Do not begin your story with long descriptions. Yes, this is boring. Just as important, this is the SAMPLE your potential readers will read before deciding not to buy your book. I have put books away because I could not get past the first chapter. Sometimes it is grammar issues, but mostly it is boring details I could live without.

If you do not know the best way to introduce excitement in the first few paragraphs, select one of the more exciting scenes in your story and splice it as a Prelim before Chapter One. It does not have to be the entire scene. It can be cut from the middle of the action, leaving the reader to wonder how did this start and where does it go.

Then introduce your characters to give your reader a chance to feel some connection, some desire to know more about them before you place them into the jaws of your plot.

Do not wait until the very end to start explaining things. They will pile up and you will be sitting there with the need to explain how your story evolved to this point. It will seem you are trying to justify the ending instead of allowing the reader to get swept up by the thrilling climax of the story.

You have to pick your moments along the way. I have gotten to where I call these moments fillers, otherwise my books would be eighty-pages of nothing but sex, space battles, and interesting looking characters. (Not necessarily in that order of importance.)

Fillers fill in my plot-line, help explain sub-plots, add depth to my characters, and provide exposition without putting the reader to sleep.

Three

It is one thing to have a couple of characters discuss technology to provide the reader with the details of how something is possible. It is more difficult to explain social constructs or histories resulting in this new world you wish to present.

Lay your groundwork early. Slip in small pieces of details whenever you can. If you know you will need to explain the political environment of your timeline, or how a war, epidemic, or global catastrophe gave rise to current events, make sure your readers become familiar with the most important facts. Refer to the epidemic in a simple conversation between friends who share the loss of parents due to the plague.

Create expressions to tell your reader something about the world-view post-major-event. "The President is more pro-AI. He thinks the problems that created the killer robots can be avoided if we try again."

When you set things up well, interjecting backstories in small bites, you will not choke your reader with a chapter on *this is what happened*. If you do find you need to fill in holes, you can do so much more quickly.

Still feel you have a lot to explain? Do not get lazy and dump it all at once. Consider a flashback. Have different parts of your exposition told by characters effected by those specific pre-events. Make it real. Ever need to sit down for a serious talk with someone and have it interrupted a half-dozen times by kids, phone calls, or other responsibilities intruding? Do a little of this between the details.

If you spread your exposition over several scenes, and/or present it from the view of different characters, your readers will be less likely to skip over important linchpins to your story's climax. They will also become more engaged.

Four

When world-building, it is important that you know everything. I keep books, journals, and notes that are constantly being updated with each new novel or short story. I have character descriptions pages long, and even graphic depictions of many of my major characters. When I write a scene with one of these characters, I often pin their image somewhere within eyesight to remind me of their personality traits.

I have a notebook with systems, stars, and distances from Earth and each other.

I have a notebook with nothing but ships and technical data -- Earth ships, alien ships, and idea ships.

There is a mythology to Space Fleet Sagas that crosses the galaxy. It is not necessary for me to share all of that with people reading my books.

As a creator of worlds, you will be tempted to describe your fully, meticulously detailed universe, with its history, intricate cultural nuances, and facts down to the habits of the minor characters. You will want to share the work you put into the research for your novel. Don't.

They do not need to know all the details of the last twelve centuries to enjoy the current situations in your current story. They certainly do not need to learn alien languages, even if you have three complete with conjugations.

Make a list of those things within your mythology *actually necessary* for the reader to follow your plot. Put in those things that add to your story. Leave out the mind-numbing unnecessary information. Save things for a sequel! Have them available for SCI-FI Conventions as discussion starters with fans. Enjoy them yourself.

Five

Despite going off track a time or two, though always on purpose, this booklet is about character development. With that in mind, if your exposition is delivered by your characters make sure those speaking know what they are talking about. If you set up a character as a communications expert, they can explain FTL communication systems. If someone has a passion for politics, they do not have to be a politician to explain the landscape. A military officer who studies battle strategies can easily discuss history, especially relative to how war shaped the current world. Your reader will buy in if you properly presented a characters experience or interests before they explain things that others do not understand as well.

People rarely tell someone something they already know. Do not have characters having conversations about old news and common knowledge (to them). Introducing a character who is an outsider but needs to be brought up-to-date. As they learn the reader learns with them. Both win.

Characters need flaws to be believed, even if they have been presented as experts. Change how the reader sees the character during longer expositions. Move the focus from the details, to more about character development.

If you are describing the current political environment, have an argument. Let one character be pro and one anti, and allow them to vent frustrations. One can be the superior type who argues with facts and figures. One can be the emotional debater, railing about injustices. Develop more layers by their opinions, but keep them friends.

With a monologue, change the focus to physical traits. Describe how lips tighten at certain descriptions. White knuckles occur when the character mentions a name. A character may be nervous with a subject and constantly giggle annoyingly.

The reader learns more about whatever you wish them to discover or accept while being entertained.

Six

Character development while presenting otherwise boring details requires a creative mind. Not just creative in world building or story telling. As a writer who wants to engage and entertain your reader, you must be creative in sliding information into the story without become narrative-heavy.

Arguments can lead to a deeper understanding of the situation and develop the relationship between the characters.

Have recent events or breaking news stream across a screen and let your characters discuss it or ignore it depending on its value to your story.

Never dismiss the value of an outsider. Someone out of the loop -- be they alien, or some geek too involved in work to keep current -- is a great questioner.

Children are invaluable to expositions on religious and philosophical constructs. If a child hears someone expose a religious or moral truth, they will question it. How it is answered, and by whom can provide context in simple terms for the child, and the reader.

What this all comes down to is learning to show instead of tell as a writer.

When you explain some of your exposition by showing something that is occurring or has happened, rather than simply detailing the events, that is writing. When a character can explain things through their personal point of view, including biases and opinions, that is writing.

My wife does not make me fearful of exposition. She makes me want to deliver boring information in creative new ways. It also taught me that I do not need nearly as much exposition as I originally believed.

You can advance your character development, add depth to a scene, and provide vital information at the same time. More essential to your future as a writer, you engage the reader.

SECTION SIX

(Originally published on Joanna Penn's blog: www.thecreativepenn.com/blog)

Four Ways To Develop Your Characters' Voices.

For a character to become believable, they must present a unique voice.

When a reader believes this person could be real, you then have the opportunity to entertain with what they actually say. Their voice is not what they say, but how they talk. A lyricist may produce a beautiful message, but if the singer is off-key, we never hang around to hear the essence of the song.

When we read a story, the characters maintain our interest. Protagonist, antagonist, and all the spear-holders move the plot along with thoughts and open dialogue. There is no overstating the importance for a writer in bringing characters alive in the reader's imagination.

Making sure each character has his or her own voice becomes key to providing the link which becomes the hook wherein the imaginary person becomes important to the reader. A writer must first provide a good story. Accepting you created a worthwhile plot, you cannot let the reader down by handing the reins to unfinished characters. The writer is tasked with producing the 'thoughts' and 'words', but you are also responsible for the voices. When we read, we 'hear' dialogue. If we do not believe the character would say what you have written, we lose interest.

1. Character Profile

A short character profile keeps you in touch with their personality. Obvious physical features can be within the profile, but a bio is the desired result. Include: Age; nationality - down to part of
country, section of city or town. Education; even grades. Work experience. Life experiences that
create changes: accidents, relationships, and relocations. Talents.

From this bio, build your character's personality. Introverted? Class clown? Opinionated? Anger issues? If you already have a vision of your character, back-build the bio to support the
personality. Either way you will discover reasons why they would or would not use certain
words.

The protagonist may use phrases popular in pop culture. A love interest who uses old-fashion phrases like 'the cat's meow." A co-worker, hesitant to join conversations, may begin with 'Not that it matters,' before expressing an opinion aloud. Keep characters consistent to keep them believable.

The more important the character, the more time spent in this practice. Not only do you become more comfortable with them, you may discover future stories hidden within the details.

Note: You do not need to share the character's bio with your readers. Let them see and hear for
themselves. It is much more entertaining.

2. Chill Your Ego

The most obvious mistake new writers make is forcing their 'wit and words' onto a main character, or worse, all of their characters. This is a nuance not often picked up by editors, almost always overlooked by the writer, and results in a failure to connect the reader to the story.

You know that guy being interviewed on television who says 'you know' after every third word, 'you know' because he uses it for filler, and 'you know' he does not realize he says 'you know' constantly 'cause, 'you know' he does it constantly? That constantly become white noise to the speaker; irritant to the listener.

I present at conferences, and during one session fell into a bad habit of finishing nearly every point with "do you get it?" This is why my wife attends these lectures. When I fall into a lazy habit, she provides a sign to make me realize what I am doing. The subtle hands to the forehead, shaking of the head, and grimace forces me to listen to myself. Once you become aware of a lazy filler or over-used phrase, making the change is simple. Making sure you do not replace one bad filler with another, equally trite alternative, is more difficult.

We all have words, phrases, and combinations so engrained in our personal use of language, we no longer 'hear' or 'see' them as out of the ordinary. Phrases like: 'at the end of the day.' 'he thought to himself.' 'and therefore.' Words we use as filler, such as: 'otherwise.' 'whatever.' 'then' and 'that.'

If you have multiple characters using the same 'unique' words and phrases, you destroy their voice with yours. You may not notice the cross-usage. There may be nothing grammatically incorrect to fix. It is not so much a failure of proper writing, as a failure to perceive words that make you feel comfortable as making someone else uncomfortable.

Let's say you use the phrase 'even so.' A character uses it in dialogue: "Even so, I do not believe we should venture into that dark cave." Another character, later, says: "Even so, the idea of cannibals in the city seems wrong."

The second character using the same phrase takes away their voice and replaces it with the first character's. It makes it difficult to separate the two, and, on a purely subconscious level, makes us not believe in either character.

There is a simple fix to this issue. Go to your main character's first spoken words. Can you perceive any words or phrases, or even word combinations even slightly odd, or, perhaps, decidedly you?

On your toolbar, select EDIT. Open FIND. In the search bar, type or paste the words. How often do they appear in your overall work? View each instance, and note how often they are part of another character's dialogue or thoughts?

When people are together for a long time, they begin to share words and phrases. Characters with long histories may do this as well. Otherwise, decide which character would most likely use that particular phrase, and make it part of his or her voice. When you FIND this phrase used by a different character, you have the opportunity for rewriting and providing this character a voice of their own.

By repeating this process, you will discover a number of words and phrases being overused and/or used by too many characters.

In changing how a character uses words and phrases, you will become a better writer. Giving each character their own speech creates personalities. Personalities connect with readers.

3. Cosplay

You do not have to dress in costume, and you do not have to have others join you, buy you should read all dialogue aloud and in character. Some will get this, and some are too uncomfortable to playact. Good actors always prepare for their roles aloud. Great actors recognize when a character is out-of-sync and brings it to the attention of the director/writers.

The very best way to hear your characters the way your readers will is to say their lines out loud.

4. Don't Be That Writer

The fourth tip is actually a way NOT to give a character voice.

Do not use italics, bold, dashes, spaces, or any other printing tool as a short-cut for creating a character's unique voice. For one, it is lazy. Secondly, it wears a reader out!

The fewer cutesy printing techniques the better. We read with our eyes, and these short-cuts break concentration. You destroy flow.

If the character has voice traits you can 'hear' as the author, but you are unsure how to get that across to the reader, in words, this presents an opportunity to learn. Read the works of another, where a character moved your emotions. Look for techniques in creative word-play you can immolate.

Fiction requires imagination. Imagination relies on the descriptions provided by the writer. Your characters are the best source to deliver your descriptions. Developing believable characters begins with providing each a unique voice.

Section Seven - Character Worksheet

No matter what anyone tells you, writing is hard work. Like any difficult job, the more preparation you have, the easier it is to produce the desired outcome. Slack off on the prep-work and the results are never as satisfying.

The Character Profile Worksheet is nothing new or revolutionary. You can fill it in as completely as you wish. Perhaps you will be more involved with your major characters and only hit the main points for minor ones. It is all up to you.

writerswrite.com has a number of worksheets that may help you organize your brave new world.

Character Profile Worksheet

<u>Basic Statistics</u>

Name:

Age:

Nationality:

Socioeconomic Level as a child:

Socioeconomic Level as an adult:

Hometown:

Current Residence: (Why the move?)

Occupation:

Income: (More than one source?)

Talents/Skills:

Birth order:

Siblings (describe relationships):

Spouse or Significant Other (describe relationship):

Children (describe relationships):

Relationship skills:

Physical Characteristics:

Height:

Weight:

Race:

Eye Color: (Glasses or Contacts)

Hair Color:

Skin color:

Shape of Face:

Distinguishing features:

How does he/she dress? (Style?)

Mannerisms:

Habits: (smoking, drinking, etc.)

Health:

Hobbies:

Favorite Sayings:

Speech patterns: (Dialect? Mumbles? Hesitates?)

Disabilities:

Greatest flaw:

Best quality:

Intellectual/Mental/Personality Attributes and Attitudes

Educational Background:

Intelligence Level:

Any Mental Illnesses?

Learning Experiences:

Character's short-term goals in life:

Character's long-term goals in life:

How does Character see himself/herself?

How does Character believe he/she is perceived by others?

How self-confident is the character?

Does the character seem ruled by emotion or logic or some combination thereof?

What would most embarrass this character?

Emotional Characteristics

Strengths/Weaknesses:

Introvert or Extrovert?

How does the character deal with anger?

With sadness?

With conflict?

With change?

With loss?

What does the character want out of life?

What would the character like to change in his/her life?

What motivates this character?

What frightens this character?

What makes this character happy?

Is the character judgmental of others?

Is the character generous or stingy?

Is the character generally polite or rude?

Spiritual Characteristics

Does the character believe in God?

What are the character's spiritual beliefs?

Is religion or spirituality a part of this character's life? If so, what role does it play?

How the Character is Involved in the Story

Character's role in the novel (main character? hero? heroine? Romantic interest?):

Scene where character first appears:

Relationships with other characters:

1. Character's Name: -- (Describe relationship with this character and changes to relationship over the course of the novel).

2. Character's Name: -- (Describe relationship with this character and changes to relationship over the course of the novel).

3. Character's Name: -- (Describe relationship with this character and changes to relationship over the course of the novel).

4. Character's Name: -- (Describe relationship with this character and changes to relationship over the course of the novel).

How this character is different at the end of the novel from when the novel began:

Additional Notes on This Character:

Me? My name is Don Foxe. Before my personal time-line became altered I had a future in academia all planned out. Earned a B.A. and two M.Ed.'s with the intention of teaching literature and or history. Even taught at a small college for a couple of semesters.

Boom. Life hit. Did pick up another undergraduate degree; a B.S. in Exercise Science. Seems a far cry from Humanities and History, but all of it revolves around teaching.

If you want to know more, try donfoxe.com. Or Google DON FOXE - FOXE with an E. I live a full life, so I take up a few pages on the search engine.

Want to discuss something or ask a question: don@donfoxe.net.

You can follow @don_foxe, but I don't tweet a lot. I read a lot of tweets because I follow some interesting people. Are you interesting?

If the guide helps, drop a review at the bookseller's on-line shop. If it sucks, drop a review at the bookseller's on-line shop. Reviews help. Best review I ever got was a one-star that made me reexamine my writing.

Should enough positive reviews occur, I'll consider another How To.

Don

June 12, 2018

www.ingramcontent.com/pod-product-compliance
Lightning Source LLC
Chambersburg PA
CBHW060618030426
42337CB00018B/3115